The Bible is a road map on how to live your life. It is the word of God, written by God through others. It was written for us, to show us there will be better days ahead, to assure us we won't end up somewhere we do not belong, to remind us to never give up and to never be afraid. Whatever we are feeling, whatever we are going through or whatever we need, we just need to turn to the Bible. God's got an answer for everything.

The Bible's exhortations, guidelines, commandments and encouragement give us very concrete and infallible insight into God's will for us in every aspect of life. The Bible is inspired by God Himself! It is His Word, containing His wisdom, His goodness, His intentions, His Judgments, His heart.

His Word also gives direct instruction to believers on answers for every need.

God's inspired and inerrant Word was given for many reasons: to teach us, rebuke us, correct us, and instruct us in righteousness; it was also given so that we may be complete and equipped for every good work. By reading the Bible on a consistent basis, you can find direction for your life and learn how to best serve the Lord who gave His life for you.

Turn to this Life Guide in any situation and it will give you an answer.

Read this guide everyday until it becomes an integral part of your life.

Table Of Contents

When You Are

Happy

Psalm 37:4

Also delight yourself in Yahweh, and he will give you the desires of your heart.

Isaiah 12:3

Therefore with joy you will draw water out of the wells of salvation.

Romans 5:2

Through whom we also have our access by faith into this grace in which we stand. We rejoice in hope of the glory of God.

Matthew 5:8

Blessed are the pure in heart, for they shall see God.

Psalm 37:4-14

Also delight yourself in Yahweh, and he will give you the desires of your heart. Commit your way to Yahweh. Trust also in him, and he will do this: he will make your righteousness shine out like light, and your justice as the noon day sun. Rest in Yahweh, and wait patiently for him. Don't fret because of him who prospers in his way, because of the man who makes wicked plots happen. Cease from anger, and forsake wrath. Don't fret; it leads only to evildoing. For evildoers shall be cut off, but those who wait for Yahweh shall inherit the land. For yet a little while, and the wicked will be no more. Yes, though you look for his place, he isn't there. But the humble shall inherit the land, and shall delight themselves in the abundance of peace. The wicked plots against the just, and gnashes at him with his teeth. The Lord will laugh at him, for he sees that his day is coming. The wicked have drawn out the sword, and have bent their bow, to cast down the poor and needy, to kill those who are upright on the path.

Ecclesiastes 3:12-13

I know that there is nothing better for them than to rejoice, and to do good as long as they live. Also that every man should eat and drink, and enjoy good in all his labor, is the gift of God.

Psalm 1:1-6

Blessed is the man who doesn't walk in the counsel of the wicked, nor stand on the path of sinners,   nor sit in the seat of scoffers; but his delight is in Yahweh's law. On his law he meditates day and night. He will be like a tree planted by the streams of water, that produces its fruit in its season,   whose leaf also does not wither. Whatever he does shall prosper. The wicked are not so, but are like the chaff which the wind drives away. Therefore the wicked shall not stand in the judgment, nor sinners in the congregation of the righteous. For Yahweh knows the way of the righteous, but the way of the wicked shall perish.

1 Peter 4:13

But because you are partakers of Christ's sufferings, rejoice, that at the revelation of his glory you also may rejoice with exceeding joy.

John 16:24

Until now, you have asked nothing in my name. Ask, and you will receive, that your joy may be made full.

Ecclesiastes 7:14

In the day of prosperity be joyful, and in the day of adversity consider; yes, God has made the one side by side with the other, to the end that man should not find out anything after him.

James 5:13

Is any among you suffering? Let him pray. Is any cheerful? Let him sing praises.

Philippians 4:4

Rejoice in the Lord always! Again I will say, "Rejoice!"

Psalm 37:4

Also delight yourself in Yahweh, and he will give you the desires of your heart.

Psalm 16:11

You will show me the path of life. In your presence is fullness of joy. In your right hand there are pleasures forever more.

Proverbs 15:13

A glad heart makes a cheerful face, but an aching heart breaks the spirit.

Matthew 25:21

"His lord said to him, 'Well done, good and faithful servant. You have been faithful over a few things, I will set you over many things. Enter into the joy of your lord.'

1 Thessalonians 3:9

For what thanksgiving can we render again to God for you, for all the joy with which we rejoice for your sakes before our God.

When You Are
Discouraged

Psalm 27:1–14

Yahweh is my light and my salvation. Whom shall I fear? Yahweh is the strength of my life. Of whom shall I be afraid? When evildoers came at me to eat up my flesh, even my adversaries and my foes, they stumbled and fell. Though an army should encamp against me, my heart shall not fear. Though war should rise against me, even then I will be confident. One thing I have asked of Yahweh, that I will seek after: that I may dwell in Yahweh's house all the days of my life, to see Yahweh's beauty, and to inquire in his temple. For in the day of trouble, he will keep me secretly in his pavilion. In the secret place of his tabernacle, he will hide me. He will lift me up on a rock. Now my head will be lifted up above my enemies around me. I will offer sacrifices of joy in his tent. I will sing, yes, I will sing praises to Yahweh. Hear, Yahweh, when I cry with my voice. Have mercy also on me, and answer me. When you said, "Seek my face," my heart said to you, "I will seek your face, Yahweh."

Don't hide your face from me. Don't put your servant away in anger.

You have been my help. Don't abandon me, neither forsake me, God of my salvation. When my father and my mother forsake me, then Yahweh will take me up. Teach me your way, Yahweh. Lead me in a straight path, because of my enemies. Don't deliver me over to the desire of my adversaries, for false witnesses have risen up against me, such as breathe out cruelty. I am still confident of this: I will see the goodness of Yahweh in the land of the living. Wait for Yahweh. Be strong, and let your heart take courage. Yes, wait for Yahweh.

Philippians 4:6–8

In nothing be anxious, but in everything, by prayer and petition with thanksgiving, let your requests be made known to God. And the peace of God, which surpasses all understanding, will guard your hearts and your thoughts in Christ Jesus. Finally, brothers, whatever things are true, whatever things are honorable, whatever things are just, whatever things are pure, whatever things are lovely, whatever things are of good report: if there is any virtue and if there is any praise, think about these things.

Isaiah 51:11

Those ransomed by Yahweh will return, and come with singing to Zion. Everlasting joy shall be on their heads. They will obtain gladness and joy. Sorrow and sighing shall flee away.

John 14:1

"Don't let your heart be troubled. Believe in God. Believe also in me."

1 Peter 1:6–9

Wherein you greatly rejoice, though now for a little while, if need be, you have been grieved in various trials, that the proof of your faith, which is more precious than gold that perishes even though it is tested by fire, may be found to result in praise, glory, and honor at the revelation of Jesus Christ— whom, not having known, you love. In him, though now you don't see him, yet believing, you rejoice greatly with joy that is unspeakable and full of glory, receiving the result of your faith, the salvation of your souls.

Psalm 31:24

Be strong, and let your heart take courage, all you who hope in Yahweh.

Hebrews 10:35–36

Therefore don't throw away your boldness, which has a great reward. For you need endurance so that, having done the will of God, you may receive the promise.

Psalm 138:7

Though I walk in the middle of trouble, you will revive me. You will stretch out your hand against the wrath of my enemies. Your right hand will save me.

Philippians 1:6

Being confident of this very thing, that he who began a good work in you will complete it until the day of Jesus Christ.

John 14:27

Peace I leave with you. My peace I give to you; not as the world gives, I give to you. Don't let your heart be troubled, neither let it be fearful.

Galatians 6:9

Let's not be weary in doing good, for we will reap in due season, if we don't give up.

2 Corinthians 4:8–9

We are pressed on every side, yet not crushed; perplexed, yet not to despair; pursued, yet not forsaken; struck down, yet not destroyed.

When You Are Lonely

Isaiah 41:10

Don't you be afraid, for I am with you. Don't be dismayed, for I am your God. I will strengthen you. Yes, I will help you. Yes, I will uphold you with the right hand of my righteousness.

Deuteronomy 4:31

For Yahweh your God is a merciful God. He will not fail you nor destroy you, nor forget the covenant of your fathers which he swore to them.

Psalm 27:10

When my father and my mother forsake me, then Yahweh will take me up.

Isaiah 54:10

For the mountains may depart, and the hills be removed; but my loving kindness will not depart from you, and my covenant of peace will not be removed," says Yahweh who has mercy on you.

Romans 8:35–39

Who shall separate us from the love of Christ? Could oppression, or anguish, or persecution, or famine, or nakedness, or peril, or sword? Even as it is written, "For your sake we are killed all day long. We were accounted as sheep for the slaughter." No, in all these things, we are more than conquerors through him who loved us. For I am persuaded that neither death, nor life, nor angels, nor principalities, nor things present, nor things to come, nor powers, nor height, nor depth, nor any other created thing will be able to separate us from God's love which is in Christ Jesus our Lord.

1 Peter 5:7

Casting all your worries on him, because he cares for you.

Psalm 147:3

He heals the broken in heart, and binds up their wounds.

Hebrews 13:5

Be free from the love of money, content with such things as you have, for he has said, "I will in no way leave you, neither will I in any way forsake you."

1 Samuel 12:22

For Yahweh will not forsake his people for his great name's sake, because it has pleased Yahweh to make you a people for himself.

Deuteronomy 31:6

Be strong and courageous. Don't be afraid or scared of them; for Yahweh your God himself is who goes with you. He will not fail you nor forsake you."

Psalm 46:1

God is our refuge and strength, a very present help in trouble.

Deuteronomy 33:27

The eternal God is your dwelling place. Underneath are the everlasting arms. He thrust out the enemy from before you, and said, 'Destroy!'

Matthew 28:20

Teaching them to observe all things that I commanded you. Behold, I am with you always, even to the end of the age." Amen.

John 14:1

"Don't let your heart be troubled. Believe in God. Believe also in me."

John 14:18

I will not leave you orphans. I will come to you.

When You Are
Dissatisfied

Psalm 63:1–5

God, you are my God. I will earnestly seek you. My soul thirsts for you. My flesh longs for you, in a dry and weary land, where there is no water. So I have seen you in the sanctuary, watching your power and your glory. Because your loving kindness is better than life, my lips shall praise you. So I will bless you while I live. I will lift up my hands in your name. My soul shall be satisfied as with the richest food. My mouth shall praise you with joyful lips.

Psalm 37:3

Trust in Yahweh, and do good. Dwell in the land, and enjoy safe pasture.

Isaiah 12:2–3

Behold, God is my salvation. I will trust, and will not be afraid; for Yah, Yahweh, is my strength and song; and he has become my salvation." Therefore with joy you will draw water out of the wells of salvation.

Isaiah 55:2

Why do you spend money for that which is not bread, and your labor for that which doesn't satisfy? Listen diligently to me, and eat that which is good, and let your soul delight itself in richness.

Psalm 103:1–5

Praise Yahweh, my soul! All that is within me, praise his holy name! Praise Yahweh, my soul, and don't forget all his benefits, who forgives all your sins, who heals all your diseases, who redeems your life from destruction, who crowns you with loving kindness and tender mercies, who satisfies your desire with good things, so that your youth is renewed like the eagle's.

Psalm 34:10

The young lions do lack, and suffer hunger, but those who seek Yahweh shall not lack any good thing.

Philippians 4:12–13

I know how to be humbled, and I also know how to abound. In everything and in all things I have learned the secret both to be filled and to be hungry, both to abound and to be in need. I can do all things through Christ, who strengthens me.

Isaiah 44:3

For I will pour water on him who is thirsty, and streams on the dry ground. I will pour my Spirit on your descendants, and my blessing on your offspring.

Psalm 107:9

For he satisfies the longing soul. He fills the hungry soul with good.

Matthew 5:6

Blessed are those who hunger and thirst for righteousness, for they shall be filled.

2 Corinthians 9:8

And God is able to make all grace abound to you, that you, always having all sufficiency in everything, may abound to every good work.

Jeremiah 31:14

"I will satiate the soul of the priests with fatness, and my people will be satisfied with my goodness," says Yahweh.

Proverbs 12:14

A man shall be satisfied with good by the fruit of his mouth. The work of a man's hands shall be rewarded to him.

Joel 2:26

You will have plenty to eat, and be satisfied, and will praise the name of Yahweh, your God, who has dealt wondrously with you; and my people will never again be disappointed.

When You Are

Tempted

Ephesians 6:10–11, 16

Finally, be strong in the Lord, and in the strength of his might. Put on the whole armor of God, that you may be able to stand against the wiles of the devil. above all, taking up the shield of faith, with which you will be able to quench all the fiery darts of the evil one.

1 Corinthians 10:12–13

In nothing be anxious, but in everything, by prayer and petition with thanksgiving, let your requests be made known to God. And the peace of God, which surpasses all understanding, will guard your hearts and your thoughts in Christ Jesus.

1 Peter 5:8–9

Be sober and self-controlled. Be watchful. Your adversary, the devil, walks around like a roaring lion, seeking whom he may devour. Withstand him steadfast in your faith, knowing that your brothers who are in the world are undergoing the same sufferings.

1 Peter 1:6–7

Wherein you greatly rejoice, though now for a little while, if need be, you have been grieved in various trials, that the proof of your faith, which is more precious than gold that perishes even though it is tested by fire, may be found to result in praise, glory, and honor at the revelation of Jesus Christ.

James 1:2–3, 12

Count it all joy, my brothers, when you fall into various temptations, knowing that the testing of your faith produces endurance. Blessed is a person who endures temptation, for when he has been approved, he will receive the crown of life, which the Lord promised to those who love him.

James 1:13–14

Let no man say when he is tempted, "I am tempted by God," for God can't be tempted by evil, and he himself tempts no one. But each one is tempted when he is drawn away by his own lust and enticed.

Hebrews 4:14–16

Having then a great high priest who has passed through the heavens, Jesus, the Son of God, let's hold tightly to our confession. For we don't have a high priest who can't be touched with the feeling of our infirmities, but one who has been in all points tempted like we are, yet without sin. Let's therefore draw near with boldness to the throne of grace, that we may receive mercy and may find grace for help in time of need.

Hebrews 2:18

For in that he himself has suffered being tempted, he is able to help those who are tempted.

1 John 1:9

If we confess our sins, he is faithful and righteous to forgive us the sins, and to cleanse us from all unrighteousness.

Jude 24–25

Now to him who is able to keep them from stumbling, and to present you faultless before the presence of his glory in great joy, to God our Savior, who alone is wise, be glory and majesty, dominion and power, both now and forever. Amen.

Proverbs 28:13

He who conceals his sins doesn't prosper, but whoever confesses and renounces them finds mercy.

Psalm 119:11

I have hidden your word in my heart, that I might not sin against you.

Romans 6:14

For sin will not have dominion over you. For you are not under law, but under grace.

1 John 4:4

You are of God, little children, and have overcome them; because greater is he who is in you than he who is in the world.

2 Peter 2:9

The Lord knows how to deliver the godly out of temptation and to keep the unrighteous under punishment for the day of judgment.

James 4:7

Be subject therefore to God. Resist the devil, and he will flee from you.

When You Are
Confused

James 3:16–18

For where jealousy and selfish ambition are, there is confusion and every evil deed. But the wisdom that is from above is first pure, then peaceful, gentle, reasonable, full of mercy and good fruits, without partiality, and without hypocrisy. Now the fruit of righteousness is sown in peace by those who make peace.

James 1:5

But if any of you lacks wisdom, let him ask of God, who gives to all liberally and without reproach, and it will be given to him.

1 Peter 4:12–13

Beloved, don't be astonished at the fiery trial which has come upon you to test you, as though a strange thing happened to you. But because you are partakers of Christ's sufferings, rejoice, that at the revelation of his glory you also may rejoice with exceeding joy.

Isaiah 43:2

When you pass through the waters, I will be with you, and through the rivers, they will not overflow you. When you walk through the fire, you will not be burned, and flame will not scorch you.

Philippians 4:6–7

In nothing be anxious, but in everything, by prayer and petition with thanksgiving, let your requests be made known to God. And the peace of God, which surpasses all understanding, will guard your hearts and your thoughts in Christ Jesus.

Psalm 55:23

But you, God, will bring them down into the pit of destruction. Bloodthirsty and deceitful men shall not live out half their days, but I will trust in you.

Isaiah 50:7

For the Lord Yahweh will help me. Therefore I have not been confounded. Therefore I have set my face like a flint, and I know that I won't be disappointed.

1 Corinthians 14:33

For God is not a God of confusion, but of peace, as in all the assemblies of the saints.

Proverbs 3:5–6

Trust in Yahweh with all your heart, and don't lean on your own understanding. In all your ways acknowledge him, and he will make your paths straight.

Isaiah 30:21

He gives power to the weak. He increases the strength of him who has no might.

2 Timothy 1:7

For God didn't give us a spirit of fear, but of power, love, and self-control.

Psalm 32:8

I will instruct you and teach you in the way which you shall go. I will counsel you with my eye on you.

Isaiah 40:29

He gives power to the weak. He increases the strength of him who has no might.

Psalm 119:165

Those who love your law have great peace. Nothing causes them to stumble.

When You Are
Worried

John 14:27

Peace I leave with you. My peace I give to you; not as the world gives, I give to you. Don't let your heart be troubled, neither let it be fearful.

Psalm 4:8

In peace I will both lay myself down and sleep, for you, Yahweh alone, make me live in safety.

Hebrews 4:3, 9

For we who have believed do enter into that rest, even as he has said, "As I swore in my wrath, they will not enter into my rest; There remains therefore a Sabbath rest for the people of God.

Colossians 3:15

And let the peace of God rule in your hearts, to which also you were called in one body, and be thankful.

Matthew 6:25–34

Therefore I tell you, don't be anxious for your life: what you will eat, or what you will drink; nor yet for your body, what you will wear. Isn't life more than food, and the body more than clothing? See the birds of the sky, that they don't sow, neither do they reap, nor gather into barns. Your heavenly Father feeds them. Aren't you of much more value than they? "Which of you by being anxious, can add one moment to his lifespan? Why are you anxious about clothing? Consider the lilies of the field, how they grow. They don't toil, neither do they spin, yet I tell you that even Solomon in all his glory was not dressed like one of these. But if God so clothes the grass of the field, which today exists and tomorrow is thrown into the oven, won't he much more clothe you, you of little faith? "Therefore don't be anxious, saying, 'What will we eat?', 'What will we drink?' or, 'With what will we be clothed?' For the Gentiles seek after all these things; for your heavenly Father knows that you need all these things. But seek first God's Kingdom and his righteousness; and all these things will be given to you as well. Therefore don't be anxious for tomorrow, for tomorrow will be anxious for itself. Each day's own evil is sufficient.

Psalm 91:1–2

He who dwells in the secret place of the Most High will rest in the shadow of the Almighty. I will say of Yahweh, "He is my refuge and my fortress; my God, in whom I trust."

Psalm 119:165

Those who love your law have great peace. Nothing causes them to stumble.

Proverbs 3:24

When you lie down, you will not be afraid. Yes, you will lie down, and your sleep will be sweet.

Philippians 4:19

My God will supply every need of yours according to his riches in glory in Christ Jesus.

John 14:1

"Don't let your heart be troubled. Believe in God. Believe also in me.

Isaiah 26:3

You will keep whoever's mind is steadfast in perfect peace, because he trusts in you.

Romans 8:6

For the mind of the flesh is death, but the mind of the Spirit is life and peace.

1 Peter 5:7

Casting all your worries on him, because he cares for you.

Philippians 4:6–7

In nothing be anxious, but in everything, by prayer and petition with thanksgiving, let your requests be made known to God. And the peace of God, which surpasses all understanding, will guard your hearts and your thoughts in Christ Jesus.

When You Feel
Guilty

Revelation 12:10–11

I heard a loud voice in heaven, saying, "Now the salvation, the power, and the Kingdom of our God, and the authority of his Christ has come; for the accuser of our brothers has been thrown down, who accuses them before our God day and night. They overcame him because of the Lamb's blood, and because of the word of their testimony. They didn't love their life, even to death.

Isaiah 55:7

Let the wicked forsake his way, and the unrighteous man his thoughts. Let him return to Yahweh, and he will have mercy on him, to our God, for he will freely pardon.

Romans 8:1

There is therefore now no condemnation to those who are in Christ Jesus, who don't walk according to the flesh, but according to the Spirit.

John 3:17–18

For God didn't send his Son into the world to judge the world, but that the world should be saved through him. He who believes in him is not judged. He who doesn't believe has been judged already, because he has not believed in the name of the one and only Son of God.

Psalm 32:5

I acknowledged my sin to you. I didn't hide my iniquity. I said, I will confess my transgressions to Yahweh, and you forgave the iniquity of my sin.

Psalm 32:1

Blessed is he whose disobedience is forgiven, whose sin is covered.

Hebrews 10:22

Let's draw near with a true heart in fullness of faith, having our hearts sprinkled from an evil conscience, and having our body washed with pure water.

Jeremiah 31:34

They will no longer each teach his neighbor, and every man teach his brother, saying, 'Know Yahweh;' for they will all know me, from their least to their greatest," says Yahweh: "for I will forgive their iniquity, and I will remember their sin no more."

1 John 1:9

If we confess our sins, he is faithful and righteous to forgive us the sins, and to cleanse us from all unrighteousness.

Isaiah 43:25

I, even I, am he who blots out your transgressions for my own sake; and I will not remember your sins.

2 Corinthians 5:17

Therefore if anyone is in Christ, he is a new creation. The old things have passed away. Behold, all things have become new.

John 8:10–11

Jesus, standing up, saw her and said, "Woman, where are your accusers? Did no one condemn you?" She said, "No one, Lord." Jesus said, "Neither do I condemn you. Go your way. From now on, sin no more."

Hebrews 8:12

For I will be merciful to their unrighteousness. I will remember their sins and lawless deeds no more."

Psalm 103:10, 12

He has not dealt with us according to our sins, nor repaid us for our iniquities. As far as the east is from the west, so far has he removed our transgressions from us.

2 Chronicles 30:9

For if you turn again to Yahweh, your brothers and your children will find compassion before those who led them captive, and will come again into this land, because Yahweh your God is gracious and merciful, and will not turn away his face from you, if you return to him."

John 5:24

"Most certainly I tell you, he who hears my word and believes him who sent me has eternal life, and doesn't come into judgment, but has passed out of death into life.

When You Are Angry

Matthew 5:22–24

But I tell you that everyone who is angry with his brother without a cause will be in danger of the judgment. Whoever says to his brother, 'Raca!' will be in danger of the council. Whoever says, 'You fool!' will be in danger of the fire of Gehenna. "If therefore you are offering your gift at the altar, and there remember that your brother has anything against you, leave your gift there before the altar, and go your way. First be reconciled to your brother, and then come and offer your gift.

Psalm 37:8

Cease from anger, and forsake wrath. Don't fret; it leads only to evildoing.

James 1:19–20

So, then, my beloved brothers, let every man be swift to hear, slow to speak, and slow to anger; for the anger of man doesn't produce the righteousness of God.

Romans 12:19

Don't seek revenge yourselves, beloved, but give place to God's wrath. For it is written, "Vengeance belongs to me; I will repay, says the Lord."

Proverbs 16:32

One who is slow to anger is better than the mighty; one who rules his spirit, than he who takes a city.

Proverbs 25:21–22

If your enemy is hungry, give him food to eat. If he is thirsty, give him water to drink; for you will heap coals of fire on his head, and Yahweh will reward you.

Proverbs 14:16–17

A wise man fears and shuns evil, but the fool is hot headed and reckless. He who is quick to become angry will commit folly, and a crafty man is hated.

Ephesians 4:31–32

Let all bitterness, wrath, anger, outcry, and slander be put away from you, with all malice. And be kind to one another, tender hearted, forgiving each other, just as God also in Christ forgave you.

Ephesians 4:26

"Be angry, and don't sin." Don't let the sun go down on your wrath.

Hebrews 10:30

For we know him who said, "Vengeance belongs to me. I will repay," says the Lord. Again, "The Lord will judge his people."

Colossians 3:8

But now you also put them all away: anger, wrath, malice, slander, and shameful speaking out of your mouth.

Proverbs 14:29

He who is slow to anger has great understanding, but he who has a quick temper displays folly.

Ecclesiastes 7:9

Don't be hasty in your spirit to be angry, for anger rests in the bosom of fools.

Matthew 6:14

"For if you forgive men their trespasses, your heavenly Father will also forgive you.

Proverbs 15:1

A gentle answer turns away wrath, but a harsh word stirs up anger.

When You Feel
Rejected

1 Chronicles 28:9

You, Solomon my son, know the God of your father, and serve him with a perfect heart and with a willing mind; for Yahweh searches all hearts, and understands all the imaginations of the thoughts. If you seek him, he will be found by you; but if you forsake him, he will cast you off forever.

Psalm 37:5–7

Commit your way to Yahweh. rust also in him, and he will do this: he will make your righteousness shine out like light, and your justice as the noon day sun. Rest in Yahweh, and wait patiently for him. Don't fret because of him who prospers in his way, because of the man who makes wicked plots happen.

1 Samuel 16:7

But Yahweh said to Samuel, "Don't look on his face, or on the height of his stature, because I have rejected him; for I don't see as man sees. For man looks at the outward appearance, but Yahweh looks at the heart."

Psalm 1:1–3

Blessed is the man who doesn't walk in the counsel of the wicked, nor stand on the path of sinners, nor sit in the seat of scoffers; but his delight is in Yahweh's law. On his law he meditates day and night. He will be like a tree planted by the streams of water, that produces its fruit in its season, whose leaf also does not wither. Whatever he does shall prosper.

1 Peter 4:16

But if one of you suffers for being a Christian, let him not be ashamed; but let him glorify God in this matter.

Matthew 5:10–12

Blessed are those who have been persecuted for righteousness' sake, for theirs is the Kingdom of Heaven. "Blessed are you when people reproach you, persecute you, and say all kinds of evil against you falsely, for my sake. Rejoice, and be exceedingly glad, for great is your reward in heaven. For that is how they persecuted the prophets who were before you.

Colossians 3:12–14

Put on therefore, as God's chosen ones, holy and beloved, a heart of compassion, kindness, lowliness, humility, and perseverance; bearing with one another, and forgiving each other, if any man has a complaint against any; even as Christ forgave you, so you also do. Above all these things, walk in love, which is the bond of perfection.

Romans 8:37

No, in all these things, we are more than conquerors through him who loved us.

Psalm 34:18

Yahweh is near to those who have a broken heart, and saves those who have a crushed spirit.

When You Are Depressed

1 Peter 4:12–13

Beloved, don't be astonished at the fiery trial which has come upon you to test you, as though a strange thing happened to you. But because you are partakers of Christ's sufferings, rejoice, that at the revelation of his glory you also may rejoice with exceeding joy.

2 Corinthians 1:3–4

Blessed be the God and Father of our Lord Jesus Christ, the Father of mercies and God of all comfort; who comforts us in all our affliction, that we may be able to comfort those who are in any affliction, through the comfort with which we ourselves are comforted by God.

1 Peter 5:6–7

Humble yourselves therefore under the mighty hand of God, that he may exalt you in due time, casting all your worries on him, because he cares for you.

Isaiah 51:11

Those ransomed by Yahweh will return, and come with singing to Zion. Everlasting joy shall be on their heads. They will obtain gladness and joy. Sorrow and sighing shall flee away.

Isaiah 41:10

Don't you be afraid, for I am with you. Don't be dismayed, for I am your God. I will strengthen you. Yes, I will help you. Yes, I will uphold you with the right hand of my righteousness.

Nehemiah 8:10

Then he said to them, "Go your way. Eat the fat, drink the sweet, and send portions to him for whom nothing is prepared, for today is holy to our Lord. Don't be grieved, for the joy of Yahweh is your strength."

Philippians 4:8

Finally, brothers, whatever things are true, whatever things are honorable, whatever things are just, whatever things are pure, whatever things are lovely, whatever things are of good report: if there is any virtue and if there is any praise, think about these things.

Isaiah 61:3

To provide for those who mourn in Zion, to give to them a garland for ashes, the oil of joy for mourning, the garment of praise for the spirit of heaviness, that they may be called trees of righteousness, the planting of Yahweh, that he may be glorified.

Isaiah 40:31

But those who wait for Yahweh will renew their strength. They will mount up with wings like eagles. They will run, and not be weary. They will walk, and not faint.

Isaiah 43:2

When you pass through the waters, I will be with you, and through the rivers, they will not overflow you. When you walk through the fire, you will not be burned, and flame will not scorch you.

Romans 8:38–39

For I am persuaded that neither death, nor life, nor angels, nor principalities, nor things present, nor things to come, nor powers, nor height, nor depth, nor any other created thing will be able to separate us from God's love which is in Christ Jesus our Lord.

Psalm 30:5

For his anger is but for a moment. His favor is for a lifetime. Weeping may stay for the night, but joy comes in the morning.

Psalm 34:17

The righteous cry, and Yahweh hears, and delivers them out of all their troubles.

Luke 18:1

He also spoke a parable to them that they must always pray, and not give up.

Psalm 147:3

He heals the broken in heart, and binds up their wounds.

When You Feel
Rebellious

1 Samuel 15:22–23

Samuel said, "Has Yahweh as great delight in burnt offerings and sacrifices, as in obeying Yahweh's voice? Behold, to obey is better than sacrifice, and to listen than the fat of rams. For rebellion is as the sin of witchcraft, and stubbornness is as idolatry and teraphim, Because you have rejected Yahweh's word, he has also rejected you from being king."

1 Peter 2:13–15

Therefore subject yourselves to every ordinance of man for the Lord's sake: whether to the king, as supreme; or to governors, as sent by him for vengeance on evildoers and for praise to those who do well. For this is the will of God, that by well-doing you should put to silence the ignorance of foolish men.

Ephesians 5:8

For you were once darkness, but are now light in the Lord. Walk as children of light.

Romans 6:12–13

Therefore don't let sin reign in your mortal body, that you should obey it in its lusts. Also, do not present your members to sin as instruments of unrighteousness, but present yourselves to God as alive from the dead, and your members as instruments of righteousness to God.

1 Peter 5:5–6

Likewise, you younger ones, be subject to the elder. Yes, all of you clothe yourselves with humility, to subject yourselves to one another; for "God resists the proud, but gives grace to the humble." Humble yourselves therefore under the mighty hand of God, that he may exalt you in due time.

Isaiah 1:19–20

If you are willing and obedient, you will eat the good of the land; but if you refuse and rebel, you will be devoured with the sword; for the Yahweh's mouth has spoken it."

Ephesians 4:17–18

This I say therefore, and testify in the Lord, that you no longer walk as the rest of the Gentiles also walk, in the futility of their mind, being darkened in their understanding, alienated from the life of God because of the ignorance that is in them, because of the hardening of their hearts.

Philippians 2:5–8

Have this in your mind, which was also in Christ Jesus, who, existing in the form of God, didn't consider equality with God a thing to be grasped, but emptied himself, taking the form of a servant, being made in the likeness of men. And being found in human form, he humbled himself, becoming obedient to the point of death, yes, the death of the cross.

Proverbs 14:16–17

A wise man fears and shuns evil, but the fool is hot headed and reckless. He who is quick to become angry will commit folly, and a crafty man is hated.

1 Peter 1:13–14

Therefore prepare your minds for action. Be sober, and set your hope fully on the grace that will be brought to you at the revelation of Jesus Christ— as children of obedience, not conforming yourselves according to your former lusts as in your ignorance.

Hebrews 5:8

Though he was a Son, yet learned obedience by the things which he suffered.

James 4:7

Be subject therefore to God. Resist the devil, and he will flee from you.

Proverbs 12:21

No mischief shall happen to the righteous, but the wicked shall be filled with evil.

Ephesians 5:21

Subjecting yourselves to one another in the fear of Christ.

Hebrews 13:17

Obey your leaders and submit to them, for they watch on behalf of your souls, as those who will give account, that they may do this with joy, and not with groaning, for that would be unprofitable for you.

What To Do When
You Are In Doubt

James 3:16–18

For where jealousy and selfish ambition are, there is confusion and every evil deed. But the wisdom that is from above is first pure, then peaceful, gentle, reasonable, full of mercy and good fruits, without partiality, and without hypocrisy. Now the fruit of righteousness is sown in peace by those who make peace.

Psalm 55:22–23

Cast your burden on Yahweh and he will sustain you. He will never allow the righteous to be moved. But you, God, will bring them down into the pit of destruction. Bloodthirsty and deceitful men shall not live out half their days, but I will trust in you.

Proverbs 29:18

Where there is no revelation, the people cast off restraint; but one who keeps the law is blessed.

Ephesians 5:1–4

Be therefore imitators of God, as beloved children. Walk in love, even as Christ also loved us and gave himself up for us, an offering and a sacrifice to God for a sweet-smelling fragrance. But sexual immorality, and all uncleanness or covetousness, let it not even be mentioned among you, as becomes saints; nor filthiness, nor foolish talking, nor jesting, which are not appropriate, but rather giving of thanks.

Proverbs 15:4

A gentle tongue is a tree of life, but deceit in it crushes the spirit.

Isaiah 43:2

When you pass through the waters, I will be with you, and through the rivers, they will not overflow you. When you walk through the fire, you will not be burned, and flame will not scorch you.

Isaiah 41:10

Don't you be afraid, for I am with you. Don't be dismayed, for I am your God. I will strengthen you. Yes, I will help you. Yes, I will uphold you with the right hand of my righteousness.

Philippians 4:6–8

In nothing be anxious, but in everything, by prayer and petition with thanksgiving, let your requests be made known to God. And the peace of God, which surpasses all understanding, will guard your hearts and your thoughts in Christ Jesus. Finally, brothers, whatever things are true, whatever things are honorable, whatever things are just, whatever things are pure, whatever things are lovely, whatever things are of good report: if there is any virtue and if there is any praise, think about these things.

Psalm 106:3

Blessed are those who keep justice. Blessed is one who does what is right at all times.

Isaiah 50:7

For the Lord Yahweh will help me. Therefore I have not been confounded. Therefore I have set my face like a flint, and I know that I won't be disappointed.

Proverbs 3:5–6

Trust in Yahweh with all your heart, and don't lean on your own understanding. In all your ways acknowledge him, and he will make your paths straight.

Psalm 30:5

For his anger is but for a moment. His favor is for a lifetime. Weeping may stay for the night, but joy comes in the morning.

Proverbs 21:23

Whoever guards his mouth and his tongue keeps his soul from troubles.

1 Peter 2:6

Because it is contained in Scripture, "Behold, I lay in Zion a chief cornerstone, chosen and precious: He who believes in him will not be disappointed."

1 Corinthians 14:33

For God is not a God of confusion, but of peace, as in all the assemblies of the saints.

Ephesians 4:29

Let no corrupt speech proceed out of your mouth, but only what is good for building others up as the need may be, that it may give grace to those who hear.

Psalm 147:3

He heals the broken in heart, and binds up their wounds.

Romans 8:38–39

For I am persuaded that neither death, nor life, nor angels, nor principalities, nor things present, nor things to come, nor powers, nor height, nor depth, nor any other created thing will be able to separate us from God's love which is in Christ Jesus our Lord.

2 Corinthians 1:3–4

Blessed be the God and Father of our Lord Jesus Christ, the Father of mercies and God of all comfort; who comforts us in all our affliction, that we may be able to comfort those who are in any affliction, through the comfort with which we ourselves are comforted by God.

Psalm 119:165

Those who love your law have great peace. Nothing causes them to stumble.

Luke 6:31

"As you would like people to do to you, do exactly so to them."

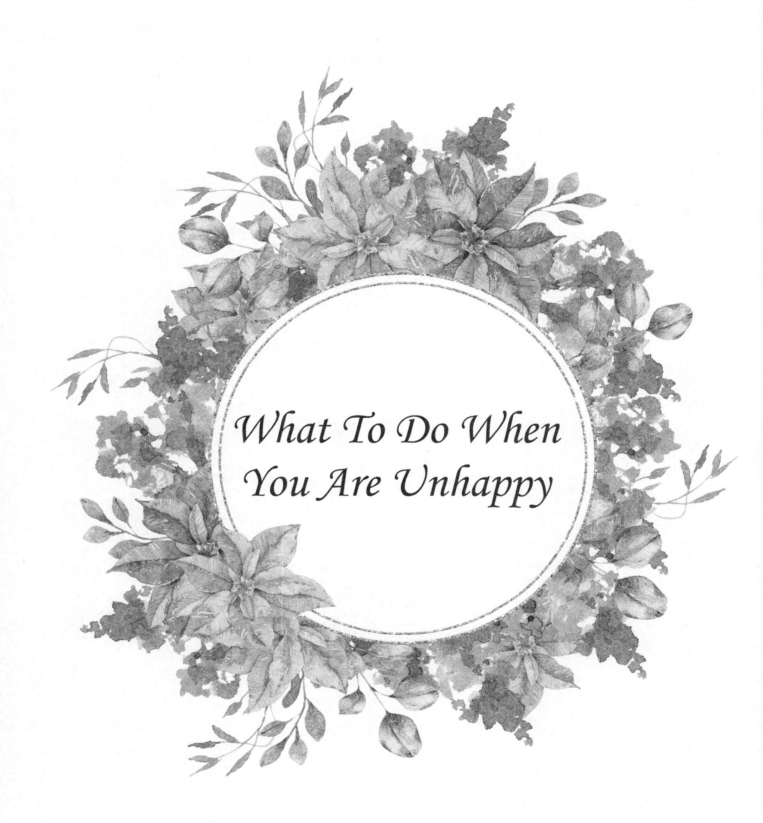

What To Do When You Are Unhappy

Psalm 37:39–40

But the salvation of the righteous is from Yahweh. He is their stronghold in the time of trouble. Yahweh helps them and rescues them. He rescues them from the wicked and saves them, because they have taken refuge in him.

Psalm 37:17–19

For the arms of the wicked shall be broken, but Yahweh upholds the righteous. Yahweh knows the days of the perfect. Their inheritance shall be forever. They shall not be disappointed in the time of evil. In the days of famine they shall be satisfied.

Romans 14:17–19

For God's Kingdom is not eating and drinking, but righteousness, peace, and joy in the Holy Spirit. For he who serves Christ in these things is acceptable to God and approved by men. So then, let's follow after things which make for peace, and things by which we may build one another up.

Psalm 119:165–169

Those who love your law have great peace. Nothing causes them to stumble. I have hoped for your salvation, Yahweh. I have done your commandments. My soul has observed your testimonies. I love them exceedingly. I have obeyed your precepts and your testimonies, for all my ways are before you.

Isaiah 55:8–9, 12

"For my thoughts are not your thoughts, and your ways are not my ways," says Yahweh. "For as the heavens are higher than the earth, so are my ways higher than your ways, and my thoughts than your thoughts.

Romans 5:1–2

Being therefore justified by faith, we have peace with God through our Lord Jesus Christ; through whom we also have our access by faith into this grace in which we stand. We rejoice in hope of the glory of God.

Isaiah 26:3–4

You will keep whoever's mind is steadfast in perfect peace, because he trusts in you. Trust in Yahweh forever; for in Yah, Yahweh, is an everlasting Rock.

Isaiah 25:8–9

He has swallowed up death forever! The Lord Yahweh will wipe away tears from off all faces. He will take the reproach of his people away from off all the earth, for Yahweh has spoken it. It shall be said in that day, "Behold, this is our God! We have waited for him, and he will save us! This is Yahweh! We have waited for him. We will be glad and rejoice in his salvation!"

Romans 15:13

Now may the God of hope fill you with all joy and peace in believing, that you may abound in hope, in the power of the Holy Spirit.

Philippians 4:6–7

In nothing be anxious, but in everything, by prayer and petition with thanksgiving, let your requests be made known to God. And the peace of God, which surpasses all understanding, will guard your hearts and your thoughts in Christ Jesus.

Romans 8:7–9

Because the mind of the flesh is hostile toward God; for it is not subject to God's law, neither indeed can it be. Those who are in the flesh can't please God. But you are not in the flesh but in the Spirit, if it is so that the Spirit of God dwells in you. But if any man doesn't have the Spirit of Christ, he is not his.

John 14:27

Peace I leave with you. My peace I give to you; not as the world gives, I give to you. Don't let your heart be troubled, neither let it be fearful.

Isaiah 57:19–21

I create the fruit of the lips: Peace, peace, to him who is far off and to him who is near," says Yahweh; "and I will heal them." But the wicked are like the troubled sea; for it can't rest and its waters cast up mire and mud. "There is no peace", says my God, "for the wicked."

2 Corinthians 4:6, 8–9

Seeing it is God who said, "Light will shine out of darkness," who has shone in our hearts to give the light of the knowledge of the glory of God in the face of Jesus Christ. We are pressed on every side, yet not crushed; perplexed, yet not to despair; pursued, yet not forsaken; struck down, yet not destroyed.

What To Do When
You Are Afraid

Psalm 91:1–2

He who dwells in the secret place of the Most High will rest in the shadow of the Almighty. I will say of Yahweh, "He is my refuge and my fortress; my God, in whom I trust."

Psalm 91:4–7

He will cover you with his feathers. Under his wings you will take refuge. His faithfulness is your shield and rampart. You shall not be afraid of the terror by night, nor of the arrow that flies by day, nor of the pestilence that walks in darkness, nor of the destruction that wastes at noonday. A thousand may fall at your side, and ten thousand at your right hand; but it will not come near you.

Psalm 56:11

I have put my trust in God. I will not be afraid. What can man do to me?

Romans 8:29, 31, 35–39

For whom he foreknew, he also predestined to be conformed to the image of his Son, that he might be the firstborn among many brothers. What then shall we say about these things? If God is for us, who can be against us? Who shall separate us from the love of Christ? Could oppression, or anguish, or persecution, or famine, or nakedness, or peril, or sword? Even as it is written, For your sake we are killed all day long. We were accounted as sheep for the slaughter." No, in all these things, we are more than conquerors through him who loved us. For I am persuaded that neither death, nor life, nor angels, nor principalities, nor things present, nor things to come, nor powers, nor height, nor depth, nor any other created thing will be able to separate us from God's love which is in Christ Jesus our Lord.

John 14:27

Peace I leave with you. My peace I give to you; not as the world gives, I give to you. Don't let your heart be troubled, neither let it be fearful.

Psalm 23:4–5

Even though I walk through the valley of the shadow of death, I will fear no evil, for you are with me. Your rod and your staff, they comfort me. You prepare a table before me in the presence of my enemies. You anoint my head with oil. My cup runs over.

Proverbs 3:25–26

Don't be afraid of sudden fear, neither of the desolation of the wicked, when it comes; for Yahweh will be your confidence, and will keep your foot from being taken.

Psalm 27:1, 3

Yahweh is my light and my salvation. Whom shall I fear? Yahweh is the strength of my life. Of whom shall I be afraid? Though an army should encamp against me, my heart shall not fear. Though war should rise against me, even then I will be confident.

Psalm 91:10–11, 14

No evil shall happen to you, neither shall any plague come near your dwelling. For he will put his angels in charge of you, to guard you in all your ways. "Because he has set his love on me, therefore I will deliver him. I will set him on high, because he has known my name.

Romans 8:15–16

For you didn't receive the spirit of bondage again to fear, but you received the Spirit of adoption, by whom we cry, "Abba! Father!" The Spirit himself testifies with our spirit that we are children of God;

Isaiah 54:14

You will be established in righteousness. You will be far from oppression, for you will not be afraid, and far from terror, for it shall not come near you.

Psalm 31:24

Be strong, and let your heart take courage, all you who hope in Yahweh.

Hebrews 13:6, 8

So that with good courage we say, The Lord is my helper. I will not fear. What can man do to me?" Jesus Christ is the same yesterday, today, and forever.

Isaiah 40:31

But those who wait for Yahweh will renew their strength. They will mount up with wings like eagles. They will run, and not be weary. They will walk, and not faint.

2 Timothy 1:7

For God didn't give us a spirit of fear, but of power, love, and self-control.

1 John 4:18

There is no fear in love; but perfect love casts out fear, because fear has punishment. He who fears is not made perfect in love.

What To Do When You Are Stressed

Romans 8:25–26

But if we hope for that which we don't see, we wait for it with patience. In the same way, the Spirit also helps our weaknesses, for we don't know how to pray as we ought. But the Spirit himself makes intercession for us with groanings which can't be uttered.

Hebrews 10:35–36

Therefore don't throw away your boldness, which has a great reward. For you need endurance so that, having done the will of God, you may receive the promise.

1 Thessalonians 5:14

We exhort you, brothers: Admonish the disorderly; encourage the faint-hearted; support the weak; be patient toward all.

Psalm 40:1

I waited patiently for Yahweh. He turned to me, and heard my cry.

James 5:7–8

Be patient therefore, brothers, until the coming of the Lord. Behold, the farmer waits for the precious fruit of the earth, being patient over it, until it receives the early and late rain. You also be patient. Establish your hearts, for the coming of the Lord is at hand.

Romans 5:3–5

Not only this, but we also rejoice in our sufferings, knowing that suffering produces perseverance; and perseverance, proven character; and proven character, hope: and hope doesn't disappoint us, because God's love has been poured into our hearts through the Holy Spirit who was given to us.

Romans 15:4–5

For whatever things were written before were written for our learning, that through perseverance and through encouragement of the Scriptures we might have hope. Now the God of perseverance and of encouragement grant you to be of the same mind with one another according to Christ Jesus.

Galatians 5:22–23

But the fruit of the Spirit is love, joy, peace, patience, kindness, goodness, faith, gentleness, and self-control. Against such things there is no law.

Hebrews 6:12

That you won't be sluggish, but imitators of those who through faith and perseverance inherited the promises.

Ecclesiastes 7:8–9

Better is the end of a thing than its beginning. The patient in spirit is better than the proud in spirit. Don't be hasty in your spirit to be angry, for anger rests in the bosom of fools.

Psalm 27:14

Wait for Yahweh. Be strong, and let your heart take courage. Yes, wait for Yahweh.

Hebrews 12:1

Therefore let's also, seeing we are surrounded by so great a cloud of witnesses, lay aside every weight and the sin which so easily entangles us, and let's run with perseverance the race that is set before us.

James 1:2–4

Count it all joy, my brothers, when you fall into various temptations, knowing that the testing of your faith produces endurance. Let endurance have its perfect work, that you may be perfect and complete, lacking in nothing.

Psalm 37:7–8, 16

Rest in Yahweh, and wait patiently for him. Don't fret because of him who prospers in his way, because of the man who makes wicked plots happen. Cease from anger, and forsake wrath. Don't fret; it leads only to evildoing.

Ephesians 4:2

With all lowliness and humility, with patience, bearing with one another in love.

Lamentations 3:25–26

Yahweh is good to those who wait for him, to the soul who seeks him. It is good that a man should hope and quietly wait for the salvation of Yahweh.

Romans 12:12

Rejoicing in hope; enduring in troubles; continuing steadfastly in prayer.

What To Do When You Are In Trouble

Isaiah 42:16

I will bring the blind by a way that they don't know. I will lead them in paths that they don't know. I will make darkness light before them, and crooked places straight. I will do these things, and I will not forsake them.

Hebrews 4:15–16

For we don't have a high priest who can't be touched with the feeling of our infirmities, but one who has been in all points tempted like we are, yet without sin. Let's therefore draw near with boldness to the throne of grace, that we may receive mercy and may find grace for help in time of need.

Isaiah 51:11

Those ransomed by Yahweh will return, and come with singing to Zion. Everlasting joy shall be on their heads. They will obtain gladness and joy. Sorrow and sighing shall flee away.

Psalm 121:1–2

I will lift up my eyes to the hills. Where does my help come from? My help comes from Yahweh, who made heaven and earth.

2 Corinthians 4:8–9

We are pressed on every side, yet not crushed; perplexed, yet not to despair; pursued, yet not forsaken; struck down, yet not destroyed.

Matthew 6:34

Therefore don't be anxious for tomorrow, for tomorrow will be anxious for itself. Each day's own evil is sufficient.

John 14:1

"Don't let your heart be troubled. Believe in God. Believe also in me."

2 Corinthians 1:3–4

Blessed be the God and Father of our Lord Jesus Christ, the Father of mercies and God of all comfort; who comforts us in all our affliction, that we may be able to comfort those who are in any affliction, through the comfort with which we ourselves are comforted by God.

Psalm 31:7

I will be glad and rejoice in your loving kindness, for you have seen my affliction. You have known my soul in adversities.

Psalm 138:7

Though I walk in the middle of trouble, you will revive me. You will stretch out your hand against the wrath of my enemies. Your right hand will save me.

1 Peter 5:7

Casting all your worries on him, because he cares for you.

Romans 8:28

We know that all things work together for good for those who love God, for those who are called according to his purpose.

Nahum 1:7

Yahweh is good, a stronghold in the day of trouble; and he knows those who take refuge in him.

Philippians 4:6–7

In nothing be anxious, but in everything, by prayer and petition with thanksgiving, let your requests be made known to God. And the peace of God, which surpasses all understanding, will guard your hearts and your thoughts in Christ Jesus.

What To Do When
You Need Money

Deuteronomy 28:2–8

All these blessings will come upon you, and overtake you, if you listen to Yahweh your God's voice. You shall be blessed in the city, and you shall be blessed in the field. You shall be blessed in the fruit of your body, the fruit of your ground, the fruit of your animals, the increase of your livestock, and the young of your flock. Your basket and your kneading trough shall be blessed. You shall be blessed when you come in, and you shall be blessed when you go out. Yahweh will cause your enemies who rise up against you to be struck before you. They will come out against you one way, and will flee before you seven ways. Yahweh will command the blessing on you in your barns, and in all that you put your hand to. He will bless you in the land which Yahweh your God gives you.

Psalm 37:23–25

A man's steps are established by Yahweh. He delights in his way. Though he stumble, he shall not fall, for Yahweh holds him up with his hand. I have been young, and now am old, yet I have not seen the righteous forsaken, nor his children begging for bread.

Deuteronomy 8:7–14, 18

For Yahweh your God brings you into a good land, a land of brooks of water, of springs, and underground water flowing into valleys and hills; a land of wheat, barley, vines, fig trees, and pomegranates; a land of olive trees and honey; a land in which you shall eat bread without scarcity, you shall not lack anything in it; a land whose stones are iron, and out of whose hills you may dig copper. You shall eat and be full, and you shall bless Yahweh your God for the good land which he has given you. Beware lest you forget Yahweh your God, in not keeping his commandments, his ordinances, and his statutes, which I command you today; lest, when you have eaten and are full, and have built fine houses and lived in them; and when your herds and your flocks multiply, and your silver and your gold is multiplied, and all that you have is multiplied; then your heart might be lifted up, and you forget Yahweh your God, who brought you out of the land of Egypt, out of the house of bondage; But you shall remember Yahweh your God, for it is he who gives you power to get wealth, that he may establish his covenant which he swore to your fathers, as it is today.

1 Timothy 6:9–10

But those who are determined to be rich fall into a temptation, a snare, and many foolish and harmful lusts, such as drown men in ruin and destruction. For the love of money is a root of all kinds of evil. Some have been led astray from the faith in their greed, and have pierced themselves through with many sorrows.

Job 41:11

Who has first given to me, that I should repay him? Everything under the heavens is mine.

1 Timothy 6:17–19

Charge those who are rich in this present world that they not be arrogant, nor have their hope set on the uncertainty of riches, but on the living God, who richly provides us with everything to enjoy; that they do good, that they be rich in good works, that they be ready to distribute, willing to share; laying up in store for themselves a good foundation against the time to come, that they may lay hold of eternal life.

Malachi 3:10–12

Bring the whole tithe into the storehouse, that there may be food in my house, and test me now in this," says Yahweh of Armies, "if I will not open you the windows of heaven, and pour you out a blessing, that there will not be room enough for. I will rebuke the devourer for your sakes, and he shall not destroy the fruits of your ground; neither shall your vine cast its fruit before its time in the field," says Yahweh of Armies. "All nations shall call you blessed, for you will be a delightful land," says Yahweh of Armies.

Matthew 6:31–33

"Therefore don't be anxious, saying, 'What will we eat?', 'What will we drink?' or, 'With what will we be clothed?' For the Gentiles seek after all these things; for your heavenly Father knows that you need all these things. But seek first God's Kingdom and his righteousness; and all these things will be given to you as well.

Proverbs 14:23

In all hard work there is profit, but the talk of the lips leads only to poverty.

Ecclesiastes 2:26

For to the man who pleases him, God gives wisdom, knowledge, and joy; but to the sinner he gives travail, to gather and to heap up, that he may give to him who pleases God. This also is vanity and a chasing after wind.

Luke 6:38

"Give, and it will be given to you: good measure, pressed down, shaken together, and running over, will be given to you. For with the same measure you measure it will be measured back to you."

Psalm 23:1

Yahweh is my shepherd: I shall lack nothing.

Matthew 6:24–25

"No one can serve two masters, for either he will hate the one and love the other, or else he will be devoted to one and despise the other. You can't serve both God and Mammon. Therefore I tell you, don't be anxious for your life: what you will eat, or what you will drink; nor yet for your body, what you will wear. Isn't life more than food, and the body more than clothing?

Proverbs 13:22

A good man leaves an inheritance to his children's children, but the wealth of the sinner is stored for the righteous.

Matthew 19:29

Everyone who has left houses, or brothers, or sisters, or father, or mother, or wife, or children, or lands, for my name's sake, will receive one hundred times, and will inherit eternal life.

2 Corinthians 9:6–8

Remember this: he who sows sparingly will also reap sparingly. He who sows bountifully will also reap bountifully. Let each man give according as he has determined in his heart, not grudgingly or under compulsion, for God loves a cheerful giver. And God is able to make all grace abound to you, that you, always having all sufficiency in everything, may abound to every good work.

Philippians 4:19

My God will supply every need of yours according to his riches in glory in Christ Jesus.

Joshua 1:8

This book of the law shall not depart from your mouth, but you shall meditate on it day and night, that you may observe to do according to all that is written in it; for then you shall make your way prosperous, and then you shall have good success.

Deuteronomy 28:11–13

Yahweh will grant you abundant prosperity in the fruit of your body, in the fruit of your livestock, and in the fruit of your ground, in the land which Yahweh swore to your fathers to give you. Yahweh will open to you his good treasure in the sky, to give the rain of your land in its season, and to bless all the work of your hand. You will lend to many nations, and you will not borrow. Yahweh will make you the head, and not the tail. You will be above only, and you will not be beneath, if you listen to the commandments of Yahweh your God which I command you today, to observe and to do.

Philippians 4:12–13

I know how to be humbled, and I also know how to abound. In everything and in all things I have learned the secret both to be filled and to be hungry, both to abound and to be in need. I can do all things through Christ, who strengthens me.

Psalm 24:1

The earth is Yahweh's, with its fullness; the world, and those who dwell in it.

Matthew 10:8

Heal the sick, cleanse the lepers, and cast out demons. Freely you received, so freely give.

1 Corinthians 16:2

On the first day of every week, let each one of you save, as he may prosper, that no collections are made when I come.

Psalm 34:10

The young lions do lack, and suffer hunger, but those who seek Yahweh shall not lack any good thing.

What To Do When
You Feel Deserted

2 Corinthians 4:9

Pursued, yet not forsaken; struck down, yet not destroyed.

Deuteronomy 31:6

Be strong and courageous. Don't be afraid or scared of them; for Yahweh your God himself is who goes with you. He will not fail you nor forsake you."

Isaiah 49:15–16

"Can a woman forget her nursing child, that she should not have compassion on the son of her womb? Yes, these may forget, yet I will not forget you! Behold, I have engraved you on the palms of my hands.

1 Samuel 12:22

For Yahweh will not forsake his people for his great name's sake, because it has pleased Yahweh to make you a people for himself.

Psalm 9:10

Those who know your name will put their trust in you, for you, Yahweh, have not forsaken those who seek you.

1 Peter 5:7

Casting all your worries on him, because he cares for you.

Isaiah 41:17

The poor and needy seek water, and there is none. Their tongue fails for thirst. I, Yahweh, will answer them. I, the God of Israel, will not forsake them.

Psalm 43:5

Why are you in despair, my soul? Why are you disturbed within me? Hope in God! For I shall still praise him: my Savior, my helper, and my God.

Psalm 91:14–15

"Because he has set his love on me, therefore I will deliver him. I will set him on high, because he has known my name. He will call on me, and I will answer him. I will be with him in trouble. I will deliver him, and honor him.

Psalm 37:25

I have been young, and now am old, yet I have not seen the righteous forsaken, nor his children begging for bread.

Psalm 27:10

When my father and my mother forsake me, then Yahweh will take me up.

Matthew 28:20

Teaching them to observe all things that I commanded you. Behold, I am with you always, even to the end of the age." Amen.

Psalm 94:14

For Yahweh won't reject his people, neither will he forsake his inheritance.

Deuteronomy 4:31

For Yahweh your God is a merciful God. He will not fail you nor destroy you, nor forget the covenant of your fathers which he swore to them.

Isaiah 62:4

You will not be called Forsaken any more, nor will your land be called Desolate any more; but you will be called Hephzibah, and your land Beulah; for Yahweh delights in you, and your land will be married.

What To Do When Nothing Is Going Right

Romans 13:13-14

Let's walk properly, as in the day; not in reveling and drunkenness, not in sexual promiscuity and lustful acts, and not in strife and jealousy. But put on the Lord Jesus Christ, and make no provision for the flesh, for its lusts.

Ephesians 5:15

Therefore watch carefully how you walk, not as unwise, but as wise.

Hebrews 3:14

For we have become partakers of Christ, if we hold the beginning of our confidence firm to the end.

Psalm 27:14

Wait for Yahweh. Be strong, and let your heart take courage. Yes, wait for Yahweh.

Isaiah 40:31

But those who wait for Yahweh will renew their strength. They will mount up with wings like eagles. They will run, and not be weary. They will walk, and not faint.

Psalm 130:5

I wait for Yahweh. My soul waits. I hope in his word.

Ephesians 5:8–11

For you were once darkness, but are now light in the Lord. Walk as children of light, for the fruit of the Spirit is in all goodness and righteousness and truth, proving what is well pleasing to the Lord. Have no fellowship with the unfruitful deeds of darkness, but rather even reprove them.

Hebrews 10:23

Let's hold fast the confession of our hope without wavering; for he who promised is faithful.

Psalm 62:5

My soul, wait in silence for God alone, for my expectation is from him.

Habakkuk 2:3

For the vision is yet for the appointed time, and it hurries toward the end, and won't prove false. Though it takes time, wait for it; because it will surely come. It won't delay.

1 John 2:28

Now, little children, remain in him, that when he appears, we may have boldness, and not be ashamed before him at his coming.

Psalm 145:15–16

The eyes of all wait for you. You give them their food in due season. You open your hand, and satisfy the desire of every living thing.

Psalm 33:20

Our soul has waited for Yahweh. He is our help and our shield.

Isaiah 25:9

It shall be said in that day, "Behold, this is our God! We have waited for him, and he will save us! This is Yahweh! We have waited for him. We will be glad and rejoice in his salvation!" It shall be said in that day, "Behold, this is our God! We have waited for him, and he will save us! This is Yahweh! We have waited for him. We will be glad and rejoice in his salvation!"

What To Do When Someone Close To You Dies

2 Corinthians 1:3–5

Blessed be the God and Father of our Lord Jesus Christ, the Father of mercies and God of all comfort; who comforts us in all our affliction, that we may be able to comfort those who are in any affliction, through the comfort with which we ourselves are comforted by God. For as the sufferings of Christ abound to us, even so our comfort also abounds through Christ.

2 Corinthians 5:8–10

We are courageous, I say, and are willing rather to be absent from the body and to be at home with the Lord. Therefore also we make it our aim, whether at home or absent, to be well pleasing to him. For we must all be revealed before the judgment seat of Christ that each one may receive the things in the body according to what he has done, whether good or bad.

1 Peter 5:7

Casting all your worries on him, because he cares for you.

1 Thessalonians 4:13–14

But we don't want you to be ignorant, brothers, concerning those who have fallen asleep, so that you don't grieve like the rest, who have no hope. For if we believe that Jesus died and rose again, even so God will bring with him those who have fallen asleep in Jesus.

Isaiah 61:1–3

The Lord Yahweh's Spirit is on me, because Yahweh has anointed me to preach good news to the humble. He has sent me to bind up the broken hearted, to proclaim liberty to the captives and release to those who are bound, to proclaim the year of Yahweh's favour and the day of vengeance of our God, to comfort all who mourn, to provide for those who mourn in Zion, to give to them a garland for ashes, the oil of joy for mourning, the garment of praise for the spirit of heaviness, that they may be called trees of righteousness, the planting of Yahweh, that he may be glorified.

1 Corinthians 15:55–57

"Death, where is your sting? Hades, where is your victory?" The sting of death is sin, and the power of sin is the law. But thanks be to God, who gives us the victory through our Lord Jesus Christ.

Isaiah 51:11

Those ransomed by Yahweh will return, and come with singing to Zion. Everlasting joy shall be on their heads. They will obtain gladness and joy. Sorrow and sighing shall flee away.

Psalm 119:41, 50

Casting all your worries on him, because he cares for you. Let your loving kindness also come to me, Yahweh, your salvation, according to your word. This is my comfort in my affliction, for your word has revived me.

2 Thessalonians 2:16–17

Now our Lord Jesus Christ himself, and God our Father, who loved us and gave us eternal comfort and good hope through grace, comfort your hearts and establish you in every good work and word.

Psalm 23:4

Even though I walk through the valley of the shadow of death, I will fear no evil, for you are with me. Your rod and your staff, they comfort me.

Isaiah 41:10

Don't you be afraid, for I am with you. Don't be dismayed, for I am your God. I will strengthen you. Yes, I will help you. Yes, I will uphold you with the right hand of my righteousness.

Matthew 5:4

Blessed are those who mourn, for they shall be comforted.

Isaiah 43:2–3

When you pass through the waters, I will be with you, and through the rivers, they will not overflow you. When you walk through the fire, you will not be burned, and flame will not scorch you. For I am Yahweh your God, the Holy One of Israel, your Savior.

Revelation 21:4

He will wipe away every tear from their eyes. Death will be no more; neither will there be mourning, nor crying, nor pain, any more. The first things have passed away."

Isaiah 49:13

For Yahweh has comforted his people, and will have compassion on his afflicted.

Hebrews 4:14–16

Having then a great high priest who has passed through the heavens, Jesus, the Son of God, let's hold tightly to our confession. For we don't have a high priest who can't be touched with the feeling of our infirmities, but one who has been in all points tempted like we are, yet without sin. Let's therefore draw near with boldness to the throne of grace, that we may receive mercy and may find grace for help in time of need.

What To Do When You Don't Understand God's Ways

Romans 8:35–37

Who shall separate us from the love of Christ? Could oppression, or anguish, or persecution, or famine, or nakedness, or peril, or sword? Even as it is written, "For your sake we are killed all day long. We were accounted as sheep for the slaughter." No, in all these things, we are more than conquerors through him who loved us.

1 Peter 4:12–13

Beloved, don't be astonished at the fiery trial which has come upon you to test you, as though a strange thing happened to you. But because you are partakers of Christ's sufferings, rejoice, that at the revelation of his glory you also may rejoice with exceeding joy.

Romans 8:28

We know that all things work together for good for those who love God, for those who are called according to his purpose.

Jeremiah 32:40

I will make an everlasting covenant with them, that I will not turn away from following them, to do them good. I will put my fear in their hearts, that they may not depart from me.

Hosea 6:1–3

"Come! Let's return to Yahweh; for he has torn us to pieces, and he will heal us; he has injured us, and he will bind up our wounds. After two days he will revive us. On the third day he will raise us up, and we will live before him. Let's acknowledge Yahweh. Let's press on to know Yahweh. As surely as the sun rises, Yahweh will appear. He will come to us like the rain, like the spring rain that waters the earth."

Psalm 55:23

But you, God, will bring them down into the pit of destruction. Bloodthirsty and deceitful men shall not live out half their days, but I will trust in you.

Isaiah 55:8–9

"For my thoughts are not your thoughts, and your ways are not my ways," says Yahweh. "For as the heavens are higher than the earth, so are my ways higher than your ways, and my thoughts than your thoughts.

1 Corinthians 10:13

No temptation has taken you except what is common to man. God is faithful, who will not allow you to be tempted above what you are able, but will with the temptation also make the way of escape, that you may be able to endure it.

Isaiah 41:10

Don't you be afraid, for I am with you. Don't be dismayed, for I am your God. I will strengthen you. Yes, I will help you. Yes, I will uphold you with the right hand of my righteousness.

Hebrews 10:23

Let's hold fast the confession of our hope without wavering; for he who promised is faithful.

Psalm 34:19

Many are the afflictions of the righteous, but Yahweh delivers him out of them all.

Jeremiah 33:3

'Call to me, and I will answer you, and will show you great and difficult things, which you don't know.'

Psalm 138:8

Yahweh will fulfill that which concerns me. Your loving kindness, Yahweh, endures forever. Don't forsake the works of your own hands.

Psalm 18:30

As for God, his way is perfect. Yahweh's word is tried. He is a shield to all those who take refuge in him.

Romans 8:31

What then shall we say about these things? If God is for us, who can be against us?

What To Do When You Don't Feel Important

Hebrews 10:35–36

Therefore don't throw away your boldness, which has a great reward. For you need endurance so that, having done the will of God, you may receive the promise.

Ephesians 3:18–19

May be strengthened to comprehend with all the saints what is the width and length and height and depth, and to know Christ's love which surpasses knowledge, that you may be filled with all the fullness of God.

Romans 8:26–27

In the same way, the Spirit also helps our weaknesses, for we don't know how to pray as we ought. But the Spirit himself makes intercession for us with groanings which can't be uttered. He who searches the hearts knows what is on the Spirit's mind, because he makes intercession for the saints according to God.

1 John 5:14–15

This is the boldness which we have toward him, that if we ask anything according to his will, he listens to us. And if we know that he listens to us, whatever we ask, we know that we have the petitions which we have asked of him.

Ephesians 3:12

In him we have boldness and access in confidence through our faith in him.

Hebrews 13:6

So that with good courage we say, "The Lord is my helper. I will not fear. What can man do to me?"

Isaiah 40:31

But those who wait for Yahweh will renew their strength. They will mount up with wings like eagles. They will run, and not be weary. They will walk, and not faint.

John 14:12

Most certainly I tell you, he who believes in me, the works that I do, he will do also; and he will do greater works than these, because I am going to my Father.

Isaiah 43:2

When you pass through the waters, I will be with you, and through the rivers, they will not overflow you. When you walk through the fire, you will not be burned, and flame will not scorch you.

Psalm 103:2–3

Praise Yahweh, my soul, and don't forget all his benefits, who forgives all your sins, who heals all your diseases.

Philippians 1:6

Being confident of this very thing, that he who began a good work in you will complete it until the day of Jesus Christ.

Philippians 4:13

I can do all things through Christ, who strengthens me.

Ephesians 4:22–23

That you put away, as concerning your former way of life, the old man that grows corrupt after the lusts of deceit, and that you be renewed in the spirit of your mind.

Zechariah 4:6

Then he answered and spoke to me, saying, "This is Yahweh's word to Zerubbabel, saying, 'Not by might, nor by power, but by my Spirit,' says Yahweh of Armies.

1 John 3:21

Beloved, if our hearts don't condemn us, we have boldness toward God.

Proverbs 3:25–26

Don't be afraid of sudden fear, neither of the desolation of the wicked, when it comes; for Yahweh will be your confidence, and will keep your foot from being taken.

What To Do When
You Are Sick

Matthew 8:8

The centurion answered, "Lord, I'm not worthy for you to come under my roof. Just say the word, and my servant will be healed.

Proverbs 4:20–22

My son, attend to my words. Turn your ear to my sayings. Let them not depart from your eyes. Keep them in the center of your heart. For they are life to those who find them, and health to their whole body.

Jeremiah 30:17

For I will restore health to you, and I will heal you of your wounds," says Yahweh; "because they have called you an outcast, saying, 'It is Zion, whom no man seeks after.'"

Psalm 103:3

Who forgives all your sins, who heals all your diseases.

Matthew 9:35

Jesus went about all the cities and the villages, teaching in their synagogues and preaching the Good News of the Kingdom, and healing every disease and every sickness among the people.

Isaiah 53:5

But he was pierced for our transgressions. He was crushed for our iniquities. The punishment that brought our peace was on him; and by his wounds we are healed.

Exodus 15:26

He said, "If you will diligently listen to Yahweh your God's voice, and will do that which is right in his eyes, and will pay attention to his commandments, and keep all his statutes, I will put none of the diseases on you which I have put on the Egyptians; for I am Yahweh who heals you."

Psalm 107:20

He sends his word, and heals them, and delivers them from their graves.

Jeremiah 17:14

Heal me, O Yahweh, and I will be healed. Save me, and I will be saved; for you are my praise.

James 5:14–15

Is any among you sick? Let him call for the elders of the assembly, and let them pray over him, anointing him with oil in the name of the Lord, and the prayer of faith will heal him who is sick, and the Lord will raise him up. If he has committed sins, he will be forgiven.

1 Peter 2:24

He himself bore our sins in his body on the tree, that we, having died to sins, might live to righteousness. You were healed by his wounds.

3 John 2

Beloved, I pray that you may prosper in all things and be healthy, even as your soul prospers.

Mark 16:17–18

These signs will accompany those who believe: in my name they will cast out demons; they will speak with new languages; they will take up serpents; and if they drink any deadly thing, it will in no way hurt them; they will lay hands on the sick, and they will recover."

Hebrews 13:8

Jesus Christ is the same yesterday, today, and forever.

Luke 6:19

All the multitude sought to touch him, for power came out of him and healed them all.

Printed in Great Britain
by Amazon

24722598R00084